D1607276

FIGHTING FORCES ON THE SEA

SUBMARINES

LYNN M. STONE

Rourke
Publishing LLC
Vero Beach, Florida 32964

www.rourkepublishing.com

PHOTO CREDITS: Cover, title page, p. 5, 6, 8, 10, 15, 16, 17, 18, 19, 21, 22, 23, 29 courtesy U.S. Navy; p. 25, 26, 27, 28 courtesy U.S. Department of Defense National Archives

Title page: *A commanding officer of a fast attack submarine looks through the periscope in the ship's control room.*

Editor: Frank Sloan

Library of Congress Cataloging-in-Publication Data

Stone, Lynn M.
  Submarines / Lynn M. Stone.
      p. cm. -- (Fighting forces on the sea)
  Includes bibliographical references and index.
  ISBN 1-59515-466-3 (hardcover)
  1. Submarines (Ships)--United States--Juvenile literature. I. Title.
  V858.S76 2006
  623.825'7--dc22

                                              2005014704

Printed in the USA

CG/CG

Rourke Publishing

www.rourkepublishing.com – sales@rourkepublishing.com
Post Office Box 3328, Vero Beach, FL 32964
1-800-394-7055

TABLE OF CONTENTS

CHAPTER 1 SUBMARINES 4

CHAPTER 2 KINDS OF SUBMARINES 14

CHAPTER 3 SUBMARINE CHARACTERISTICS 20

CHAPTER 4 EARLY HISTORY 24

CHAPTER 5 WORLD WAR II 26

CHAPTER 6 AFTER WORLD WAR II 28

CHAPTER 7 THE FUTURE OF SUBMARINES 29

GLOSSARY 30

INDEX 32

FURTHER READING/WEBSITES TO VISIT 32

SUBMARINES

The modern submarine is one of the most complex and **lethal** weapons ever devised. Like a great shark, it can lurk deep in the ocean, travel swiftly and silently, and then deliver a sudden, crushing blow to any opponent. Unlike earlier submarines, modern American submarines are **nuclear**-powered. Nuclear submarines can remain underwater for months at a time, cruising secretly and stealthily throughout the oceans, even under polar ice packs. They have built-in systems to make oxygen for their crews, and the nuclear engines do not need oxygen. Earlier submarines had to surface for fresh air to recharge their batteries. On top of the sea, they were easy targets for surface warships and patrol planes.

▲

The Jimmy Carter is an extended hull Seawolf-class attack submarine. The longer hull will provide the room necessary for testing a new generation of weapons, sensors, and undersea vehicles.

The attack submarine USS Columbus *conducts an emergency surface training exercise off the coast of Oahu, Hawaii.*

A submarine dives by filling its **stern** and **bow** ballast tanks with water, which quickly adds additional weight. It can dive over 100 feet (30.5 meters) in less than a minute, and it can safely reach depths around 1,300 feet (396 meters). A submarine dive is limited by the amount of water pressure its **hull** can tolerate. The sub lightens itself for returning to the surface by blowing water out.

America's nuclear submarines spend nearly all of their operational time undersea, where they can travel at speeds over 30 knots (35 miles, 56 kilometers per hour).

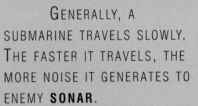

FACT FILE ★

GENERALLY, A SUBMARINE TRAVELS SLOWLY. THE FASTER IT TRAVELS, THE MORE NOISE IT GENERATES TO ENEMY **SONAR**.

In this painting, a new Virginia-class attack submarine fires a torpedo. The first Virginia-class warship was delivered to the U.S. Navy in 2004.

A submarine's crew in the darkness of the deep ocean knows its location through a built-in guidance system. Navigational charts and sonar help a submarine commander recognize dangerous underwater obstacles. Inaccurate charts can be life-threatening for a submarine, especially if the ship's sonar is inactive.

▲

A Navy lieutenant watches the console in the control room of the fast attack submarine USS Hampton *on its way to the North Pole.*

Submariners themselves—about 140 per ship—are almost as unusual as the ships on which they serve. They are twice-over volunteers—volunteers within the all-volunteer U.S. Military. They work in a unique and highly confined environment, like a windowless, three-story building just 30 feet (9 meters) wide, in spaces surrounded by technology. And they are aboard for two or more months at a time.

SUBMARINE SPECIFICATIONS

Ballistic Missile Submarines - SSBN (*Ohio* class)

Powerplant:
One nuclear reactor, one shaft

Length:
560 feet (171 meters)

Beam:
42 feet (13 meters)

Displacement:
18,750 tons (17,063 metric tons) submerged

Speed:
20+ knots (23+ miles, 37+ kilometers per hour)

Ship's company:
15 officers, 140 enlisted

Armament:
24 tubes for Trident I and II, MK-48 torpedoes, four torpedo tubes

Commissioning date, first ship:
1981

Attack Submarines – SSN (*Los Angeles* class)

Powerplant:
One nuclear reactor, one shaft

Length:
360 feet (110 meters)

Beam:
33 feet (10 meters)

Displacement:
6,900 tons (6,279 metric tons) submerged

Speed:
20+ knots (23+ miles, 37+ kilometers per hour)

Ship's company:
13 officers, 121 enlisted

Armament:
Tomahawk missiles, VLS tubes (SSN 719 and later); MK-48 torpedoes, four torpedo tubes

Commissioning date, first ship:
1976

SUBMARINE SPECIFICATIONS

Attack Submarines – SSN (*Seawolf* class)

Powerplant:
One nuclear reactor, one shaft

Length:
Seawolf and *Connecticut* 353 feet (108 meters); *Jimmy Carter* 453 feet (138 meters)

Beam:
40 feet (12 meters)

Displacement:
Seawolf and *Connecticut* 9,138 tons (8,448 metric tons); *Jimmy Carter* 12,158 tons (11,391 metric tons) submerged

Speed:
25+ knots (28+ miles, 46+ kilometers per hour)

Ship's company:
14 officers, 126 enlisted

Armament:
Tomahawk missiles; MK-48 torpedoes, 8 torpedo tubes

Commissioning date, first ship:
1997

Attack Submarines – SSN (*Virginia* class)

Powerplant:
One nuclear reactor, one shaft

Length:
377 feet (115 meters)

Beam:
34 feet (10.4 meters)

Displacement:
7,800 tons (7,098 metric tons) submerged

Speed:
25+ knots (28+ miles, 46+ kilometers per hour)

Ship's company:
14 officers, 120 enlisted

Armament:
Tomahawk missiles, 12 VLS tubes; MK-48 ADCAP torpedoes, 4 torpedo tubes

Commissioning date, first ship:
2004

KINDS OF SUBMARINES

Ohio-**class** ballistic missile submarines, sometimes called Trident submarines, carry long-range strategic Trident missiles. Trident submarines are designed to attack military bases and cities from the sea. Their long-range missiles can hit targets from 1,500 to 4,000 miles (2,400 to 6,400 kilometers) distant. A ballistic submarine could hit New York City, for example, with a missile launched from the Pacific Ocean about 1,500 miles (2,400 kilometers) west of Los Angeles! The missiles are fired through launching tubes in the submarine hull.

An Ohio-class Trident submarine cruises off the Bahama Islands.

These submarines represent one of America's greatest **deterrents** to nuclear attack from any potential enemy. Any aggressor would risk not only a **retaliatory** attack from American land-based missiles, but also from concealed Trident subs as well.

The four oldest of the 18 *Ohio*-class submarines are being converted to guided missile submarines (SSGN). These ships will be armed with up to 154 Tomahawk or Tactical Tomahawk land attack missiles. They will also be able to carry up to 66 Special Forces troops. Equally important, the SSGN subs can support the Special Forces up to 90 days. SSN subs outfitted for Special Forces are limited to two-week support operations.

◄*One of the four* Ohio-*class submarines being converted to a guided-missile warship, the USS Ohio undergoes work at Puget Sound Naval Shipyard, Bremerton, Washington, in 2004.*

Armed with a variety of weapons, including Tomahawk missiles, attack submarines are designed largely to seek and destroy enemy ships, including enemy submarines. The ships are equipped with sonar (sound navigation and ranging system), **periscopes**, and radar to identify surface ships. The Navy has 51 attack submarines in the *Los Angeles* class, the first of which was the USS *Los Angeles*. *Los Angeles* was **commissioned** in 1976. The 360-foot (110-meter) long *Los Angeles* submarines are the backbone of the Navy's attack subs.

Three curious polar bears approach the bow of the Los Angeles-*class attack submarine* Honolulu. *Not invited aboard, the three bears wandered away after a two-hour wait.*

The Navy also has three *Seawolf*-class attack submarines, which are newer, quieter, and faster than the *Los Angeles* class. They were designed to be the ultimate deep-water submarine hunters when the United States was concerned about the threat of Soviet nuclear submarines. The USS *Seawolf*, the first of the class, was commissioned in 1997. The newest of the three ships is the USS *Jimmy Carter*. It is considerably longer (453 feet to 353 feet, 138 meters to 108 meters) than its classmates. While the *Jimmy Carter* will operate as an attack sub, the Navy is also using its larger size to test new technologies and equipment.

▲
The longest of the Seawolf-*class attack submarines,* Jimmy Carter *was commissioned by the U.S. Navy in 2005.*

The newest class of attack submarines, the 377-foot (115-meter) long *Virginia* class, is designed for shallow water warfare as well as deep sea operations. The first of the class, the USS *Virginia*, was delivered to the Navy in 2004. Eventually, the Navy may have 30 *Virginia* class submarines.

▲

The USS Virginia *returns to the General Dynamics Electric Boat shipyard in Groton, Connecticut, following its first voyage in open seas during summer, 2004.*

Submarine Characteristics

A submarine is long and rounded, like a cigar with a teardrop head. That shape slices more easily through an undersea, all-water environment than through a water-and-air environment, which a sub encounters on the ocean surface. Modern American submarines can actually travel faster under water, their primary environment, than on the surface. Even the first American nuclear sub, the *Nautilus*, was designed with a narrow bow for more surface speed.

▲
Almost like a steel cigar, the nuclear-powered attack submarine USS Albany *slips through Chesapeake Bay after a six-month mission.*

A submarine's streamlined hull is made of titanium, a very strong but lightweight metal. The smooth flow of the hull is interrupted by the submarine's sail, or conning tower, the tall, slender structure that rises from the submarine hull. About 20 feet (6 meters) tall, the sail houses periscopes and radar and radio equipment. The submarine captain uses the top of the sail as a command bridge when the ship is on the ocean surface.

▲
A submarine's sail, or conning tower, houses its periscope and much of its electronic systems.

The nuclear energy that powers a submarine allows a sub to stay on patrol almost indefinitely. If necessary, it can spend up to six months submerged, returning to base only for food and supplies. As the Navy says, "There's no need to stop for gas." The nuclear material of a submarine needs to be replaced only once or twice in the ship's lifetime.

▲

The crews of the attack submarine USS Hampton and Great Britain's attack submarine Tireless met on the ice of the North Pole along with scientists from both ships.

EARLY HISTORY

The possibility of undersea travel captured imaginations long before it became a reality. A Dutch scientist in 1620 managed to submerge a rowboat covered with waterproof hides—without killing himself.

American David Bushnell designed the *Turtle*, a one-man **submersible**. The *Turtle* attempted to sink a British warship in New York Harbor in 1776, but this first known attack by submarine failed.

During the Civil War (1861-1865), another one-man submersible, the Confederate *Hunley*, succeeded in sinking the Union *Housatonic*. But the *Hunley* sank itself in the process. (In 2000 the *Hunley* was raised from the bottom of Charleston Harbor for repair and museum display.)

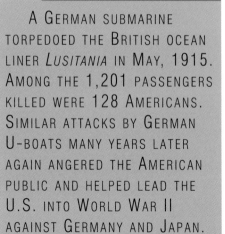

FACT FILE ★

A GERMAN SUBMARINE TORPEDOED THE BRITISH OCEAN LINER *LUSITANIA* IN MAY, 1915. AMONG THE 1,201 PASSENGERS KILLED WERE 128 AMERICANS. SIMILAR ATTACKS BY GERMAN U-BOATS MANY YEARS LATER AGAIN ANGERED THE AMERICAN PUBLIC AND HELPED LEAD THE U.S. INTO WORLD WAR II AGAINST GERMANY AND JAPAN.

The first somewhat reliable American submarine was the invention of John Holland. It could travel 6 knots (7 miles, 11 kilometers) per hour under water. Named the USS *Holland*, it was added to the Navy fleet in 1900.

But in the next few years, Germany led the way in submarine development. Germany's **Unterseeboote**, or U-boats, became a deadly menace to surface ships as World War I (1914-1918) unfolded.

After America's entry into the war in 1917, U.S. submarines were used largely to patrol American coasts. After the war, American designers made improvements in their submarines by studying the much more reliable German subs.

▲

Survivors of a German U-Boat attack in April, 1918, are rescued by a passing ship.

WORLD WAR II

America's undersea war was fought largely against the Japanese, and it was a major success. American subs sank over 30 percent of the Japanese Navy and over half of its merchant ships, a total of 1,314

military and merchant ships, including 8 Japanese aircraft carriers and almost 5 million tons (4.6 million metric tons) of shipping.

▲
An officer of a World War II submarine steadies the periscope in 1942.

Submarines also carried World War II raiders (similar to the Special Forces of today) to enemy shores, laid **mines**, and rescued downed flyers and shipwreck survivors. Fifty-two American subs were lost along with 3,506 submariners, all of them—then, as now—volunteers.

▲

The USS Robalo *is shown at her launching on May 9, 1943, into Lake Michigan. A little more than a year later, on patrol in the Pacific, the* Robalo *disappeared, possibly the victim of a mine.*

CHAPTER SIX

AFTER WORLD WAR II

The *Nautilus*, launched in 1954, was revolutionary. As the first nuclear-powered submarine, it broke all existing speed and endurance records for submarines.

In the late 1950s the U.S. Navy developed the first ballistic missile submarines. By 1981, the United States had launched the first of the big (560-foot, 171-meter), Trident-carrying *Ohio*-class submarines.

American attack submarines fired cruise missiles at targets in Iraq and in Serbia during conflicts in the 1990s.

▲

The USS Albacore, *shown here in 1954, introduced the revolutionary teardrop submarine shape.*

THE FUTURE OF SUBMARINES

Submarine technology changes quickly. Ships already under construction cannot always accommodate the new technology. But the Navy plans to build its newest *Virginia*-class submarines with a modular design that will permit easier replacement of outdated equipment and systems.

Meanwhile, depending upon the relations between the United States and other nations, the total attack submarine force will gradually shrink, perhaps to as few as 37. American submarines of the future may rely on smaller crews and even unmanned ships. As always, the Navy will emphasize technology and sea warfare superiority over numbers of ships.

▲

An artist's head-on view shows the newest of the U.S. Navy's fast attack Virginia-class *submarines in its undersea environment.*

Glossary

bow (BAU) — the front part of a ship

class (KLAS) — a group of ships manufactured to the same, or very similar, specifications, such as the *Seawolf* class of American submarines

commissioned (kuh MISH und) — to have officially been placed into service by the U.S. Navy

deterrents (duh TUR untz) — things that act as reasons not to do something

hull (HUL) — the main frame and body of a ship

lethal (LEE thul) — deadly

mines (MYNZ) — explosive devices planted on or near the ocean surface and triggered when struck by a ship

nuclear (NYU klee ur) — providing atomic energy in a controlled, but powerful way

periscopes (PAIR uh SCOPZ) — tube-like apparatuses that rise from a submarine conning tower and allow a submerged submarine crew to view the ocean surface

retaliatory (ruh TAL yuh TOR ee) — striking back at someone or something after first being struck

sonar (SOH NAR) — a system in which the echoes of controlled sound waves are used to measure distances and shapes undersea

stern (STURN) — the rear part of a ship

submersible (sub MUR suh bul) — a vessel such as a submarine, that can sail underwater

unterseeboote (OON tur zay BOT uh) — the name for German submarines, first used in World War I

INDEX

attack submarines   17, 18, 19, 28

ballast tanks   7

ballistic missile submarines   14, 28

crews   4, 9, 29

guided missile submarines   16

Holland, John   25

hull   7, 14, 22

Hunley   24

Los Angeles class   12, 17

missiles   14, 16, 17

nuclear energy   23

Ohio class   12, 14, 16, 28

periscopes   17, 22

Seawolf class   13, 18

Special Forces   16

submarines   11, 27

USS *Nautilus*   20, 28

Virginia class   13, 19, 29

World War I   25

World War II   26, 27

FURTHER READING

Green, Michael and Gladys. *Attack Submarines: The Seawolf Class*. Edge Books, 2004

Mallard, Neil. *Submarine*. DK Books, 2003

Payan, Gregory. *Life on a Submarine*. Scholastic, 2000

Woodford, Chris. *Ships and Submarines*. Facts on File, 2004

WEBSITES TO VISIT

http://www.chinfo.navy.mil/navpalib/ships/submarines

http://www.pbs.org/wgbh/nova/subsecrets

http://americanhistory.si.edu/subs

ABOUT THE AUTHOR

Lynn M. Stone is the author and photographer of many children's books. Lynn is a former teacher who travels worldwide to pursue his varied interests.